Foreword

Owning a puppy can be incredibly rewarding and a great source of companionship. Pets can provide opportunities for social interactions, helping people feel less lonely and isolated. Growing up with pets also offers health benefits, and caring for an animal can help improve a child's social skills, encouraging the development of compassion, understanding and a respect for living things. Having a puppy is, however, a huge responsibility and requires long-term commitment in terms of care and finances.

Before getting a puppy, it is important that time is taken to discuss the commitment and care required with all family members, and that everyone agrees to having and looking after a puppy in the home. Bear in mind that once you have your puppy there is a legal requirement under the Animal Welfare Act 2006 to care for them properly, so you must be sure that you will be able to do this throughout your puppy's life. This means providing somewhere suitable for them to live, a healthy diet, opportunities to behave normally, the provision of appropriate company, and ensuring that they are well.

If you are able to care for a puppy properly and make the decision to go ahead, then please consider giving a home to one of the many puppies currently in the RSPCA's animal centres throughout England and Wales.

This book is based on up-to-date knowledge of dog behaviour and welfare approved by the RSPCA. It has been written to provide you with all the care information you need to keep your puppy happy and healthy throughout your lives together. We hope you enjoy it.

Samantha Gaines BSc (Hons) MSc PhD
Alice Potter BSc (Hons) MSc
Lisa Richards BSc (Hons)
Jane Tyson BSc (Hons) MSc PhD
Animal behaviour and welfare experts, Companion
Animals Department, RSPCA

Introduction

Owning and caring for a dog can be great fun and very rewarding. It is also a big responsibility and a long-term commitment. Typically, dogs live for around 12 years, but some may live much longer, so before you get a puppy here are some of the things you need to consider:

Keeping a dog is costly

There is the initial expense of the puppy and everything they will need, such as toys and bedding. There are also long-term costs you should budget for, such as food, insurance, the cost of boarding kennels or pet sitters when you go on holiday, and veterinary care, which includes vaccinations.

Dogs need space

Before you commit, consider whether you have enough space for a dog. All dogs, even small ones, need exercise and somewhere they can rest undisturbed. So have a think about whether there is space in your house (and also in your car), and if there are suitable places where you can take your dog for regular exercise.

Dogs need company

Will a dog fit in with your lifestyle? Can you be around so your pet is not left alone for long periods, and can you put aside enough time each day for walks, training, play and everything else your puppy needs?

The right type of dog for your family and lifestyle

Take time to find out which type of dog will fit best into your family. While you may have a preference regarding the breed, size or sex, remember that every dog is unique. How a puppy behaves and fits into your family will depend on how they are treated and trained, as well as their character and temperament.

The Animal Welfare Act

Under the Animal Welfare Act 2006 it is a legal obligation to care for animals properly by meeting five welfare needs. These are: a suitable place to live, a healthy diet including clean, fresh water, the ability to behave normally, appropriate company, and protection from pain, injury and illness. This care guide contains lots of information and tips to help you make sure these needs are met.

LIFE HISTORY

SCIENTIFIC NAME
Canis familiaris

GESTATION PERIOD
63 days (approx.)

LITTER SIZE
Varies, average of 6 (approx.)

EYES OPEN
10–14 days (approx.)

WEANING AGE
From 3–4 weeks of age, puppies can be offered small amounts of moistened food in addition to their mother's milk. They can be fully weaned at about 8 weeks.

PUBERTY
Varies with size and type of dog, 6–12 months

ADULT WEIGHT
Varies greatly, can be up to 70kg (150lbs) (approx.)

LIFE EXPECTANCY
12 years (average)

FAR LEFT: Eight-week-old crossbreed puppies. RIGHT: Twelve-week-old tri-coloured Collie.

Choosing the right type of dog for you

If you are certain that you will be able to care for a puppy, the next stage is to do plenty of research to decide which type of dog is right for you.

EXTRA-LARGE AND LARGE DOGS

Afghan Hound
Borzoi
Boxer
Bullmastiff
Chow Chow
Dalmatian
Deerhound
Dobermann
German Shepherd Dog (illustrated)
Giant Schnauzer
Great Dane
Greyhound
Irish Setter
Mastiff

Newfoundland
Old English Sheepdog
Pointer and German Pointer
Poodle (Standard)
Pyrenean Mountain Dog
Retriever (including Labrador)
Rhodesian Ridgeback
Rottweiler
Saluki
Weimaraner

MEDIUM-SIZE DOGS

Australian Cattle Dog
Beagle
Collie and Border Collie
Keeshond
Poodle (Miniature)
Shetland Sheepdog
Spaniel (e.g. English Springer (illustrated), Welsh Springer, Sussex)

Staffordshire Bull Terrier
Terrier (e.g. Irish, Kerry Blue, Soft-Coated Wheaten)
Whippet

Sex

Personal taste apart, there is very little significance in the choice between a male and a female puppy, as both can make excellent pets. Both sexes will require neutering to avoid unwanted pregnancies. Neutering can also reduce behaviours such as roaming and urine marking in male dogs, and prevents females from attracting unwanted attention when they come into season. It can also have health benefits for your dog. There is no need for a female to have a litter before she is neutered. Speak to your vet about the best time to neuter your dog.

Size

Dogs vary in size more than any other pet animal, even within breeds, so this is an important consideration when choosing a dog. It is easily overlooked when you are looking at a litter of tiny puppies, but remember that some breeds of dog can grow into adults weighing as much as 70kg (150lbs). Whatever their size, all dogs need space in which to relax, play and exercise. The following is only a very general guide with examples:

SMALL DOGS

Dachshund (Miniature Long-haired)

Poodle (Toy)

Schipperke

Schnauzer (Miniature)

Shih Tzu

Terrier (e.g. Australian, West Highland White (illustrated), Border Cairn)

TOY DOGS

Chihuahua

Griffons Bruxellois

Italian Greyhound

Japanese Chin

Maltese

Miniature Pinscher

Papillon

Pekingese

Pomeranian (illustrated)

Spaniel (e.g. Cavalier King Charles, King Charles)

Terrier (e.g. Australian Silky, English Toy, Yorkshire)

Types of dog

Over the centuries, different types of dog have been bred for specific purposes, so people tend to think of some types as being 'family dogs' or 'easy to train'. Others like a particular type because of their looks. Both factors often influence people when they are choosing a dog. Keep in mind, however, that you need to look beyond these generalizations, as every dog has their own unique character and temperament. The way they behave will depend upon how they are reared, treated and trained.

Dogs are generally classified by type into certain groups, but regardless of what they were bred for, all dogs need exercise, training and appropriate care.

Purebred or crossbreed

Whether you decide to buy a purebred dog (the dog's parents are both the same single breed) or a crossbreed (a mix of two or more breeds), there is a huge variety to choose from. There are advantages to both of these, and your decision may depend upon your personal choice, your situation and the circumstances of the puppies you are considering. When buying puppies that the breeders have registered as pedigrees, you will have a better idea of their parentage and what to expect in terms of their adult appearance. Genetic testing may also have been carried out to ensure that puppies are not predisposed to particular conditions.

On the other hand, crossbreeds are less likely to show the exaggerated physical features and inherited diseases present in particular breeds, although they can still inherit disorders from their parents' breeds. They also generally cost less to buy and are cheaper to insure. Whatever type of dog you're thinking of getting, it's important to find out what health and physical issues they may be vulnerable to developing. Quite apart from your puppy's pain and suffering, you may face expensive bills for veterinary treatment. Knowing which types of dogs tend to have fewer problems will give you the best chance of getting a happy, healthy puppy.

Hounds

Hounds were originally used for hunting, either by sight or by scent, but many are kept successfully as pets and can live with other animals. Sight hounds include the Afghan Hound, Borzoi, Greyhound and Saluki. Scent hounds include the Beagle and Bloodhound.

Terriers

These are typically the smallest of the hunting breeds. Terrier breeds include the Airedale, Border, Irish, Kerry Blue, Lakeland, Scottish, Skye, Welsh and West Highland White.

Gundogs

These dogs were originally trained to find, point and retrieve game, usually gamebirds, including waterfowl. Gundogs include Setters, Pointers, Retrievers and Spaniels. Of these, the Labrador Retriever tends to be the most popular pet.

Working dogs

These include dogs originally bred to do a range of jobs, including guarding, and search and rescue, although many are now kept primarily as family pets. The group includes the Boxer, Bullmastiff and Rottweiler; polar breeds, such as the Alaskan Malamute, Samoyed and Siberian Husky; and search and rescue breeds, such as the St Bernard and the Newfoundland.

Pastoral dogs

This group consists of dogs originally bred for herding cattle, sheep, reindeer and other animals. It includes breeds of various sizes, such as the Collie family, the Finnish Lapphund, and sheepdogs, including the Old English and Maremma Sheepdog.

Utility dogs

Utility dogs are those breeds that are not included in the sporting or working categories above, but were once bred for a particular role, although as with dogs from other groups, many are now successfully kept as pets. Members of this group include the Akita, Dalmatian, Keeshond, Poodle and Schnauzer.

Toy dogs

Many toy breeds were bred to be companion or lap dogs, although like all dogs they require exercise and training. Some well-known toy breeds include the Chihuahua, Maltese, Papillon, Pekingese, Pomeranian, Pug and Yorkshire Terrier. Because of their small size, these dogs can be vulnerable to injury.

CLOCKWISE FROM TOP LEFT: Pastoral dogs: Border Collie cross; Utility dogs: Schnauzer; Working dogs: Dobermann; Toy dogs: Chihuahua; Terriers: Border Terrier; Gundogs: Labrador Retriever; Hounds: Lurcher.

Buying a puppy

Where to buy

Although you may have decided what size, sex and type of dog is most suitable for your family, you should take your time in selecting the right puppy.

Rehoming charities such as the RSPCA often have puppies as well as adult dogs available. They may have both crossbreed and purebred puppies of all shapes and sizes.

If you buy your puppy directly from the person who bred them, do some research first. For example, look for responsible breeders who screen the puppies' parents to detect inherited diseases. Breeders should be happy to discuss with you issues such as how the puppies have been kept, and invite you to visit them to meet the parents and puppies.

Never buy puppies from a puppy farm, where they are bred for sale in large numbers and are more likely to have major health and behavioural problems throughout their lives. Also avoid advertisements that invite you to meet the breeder to collect the puppy at any place other than where the puppy was born. You will be unable to see where the puppy has come from, as well as the behaviour and health of its parents.

Although pet shops are regulated by local authorities, you should not buy a puppy if you have no way of telling what the origin of the puppy is, and are unable to see the place they came from or its parents and siblings.

Meeting a puppy

Before you go to see a puppy it is a good idea to call the breeder and ask relevant questions. You can find out more about what to ask at www.getpuppysmart.com/questions_for_breeder. When you are choosing a puppy make sure that you see the litter with their mother and look for signs that the puppies seem healthy and well cared for. It is helpful to take along other adult members of your family so you can watch to see how the puppies interact with you all. If the puppies seem nervous or timid, they may not have had enough chances to socialize; this could mean that they will be scared or anxious as they grow older, particularly around strangers and other dogs. If you have any doubts about a litter, it is best not to choose one of the puppies as your pet. Never pick a timid puppy because you feel sorry for them.

Documentation

When you are buying a puppy it is a good idea to use the 'puppy contract', which includes a puppy information pack. This is available to download at www.puppycontract.org.uk. Sellers fill in background details about the puppy's parents and any health issues, plus sections on everything from the puppy's vaccination and worming record to whether they have been microchipped, the puppy's current weight

and diet, and details on how the puppy has been socialized. This all helps the buyer make an informed decision about whether they want to buy the puppy. In return, the buyer agrees in the contract that they intend to care for the puppy and ensure that all their needs are met.

Finding a healthy puppy

Whether you meet your puppy in a rehoming centre or at a breeder's home, you should always check that they are healthy. Here are some of the things that may be signs that the puppy has an underlying medical problem:

- Visible ribs
- Dull, scruffy coat
- Sore patches of skin
- Red eyes
- Runny eyes or nose
- Coughing
- Signs of diarrhoea around the tail/bottom
- Signs of external parasites (e.g. fleas), such as scratching, areas of hair loss, or thickened

skin in areas like around the ear edges.
- Weakness, wobbliness or difficulty standing up
- Becoming tired very quickly during interaction or play
- Noisy or laboured breathing
- Limping, difficulty walking or lifting legs
- A prolonged hunched or crouched body posture
- Straining when passing urine or faeces

These are just a few examples. If you notice anything at all that doesn't look quite right with the puppies you have seen, you may want to consider getting your puppy from somewhere else. If you have concerns about any of the animals you have seen, call the RSPCA (details can be found at www.rspca.org.uk).

TOP LEFT: These dogs at the RSPCA Animal Centre in Leybourne are just two of the many animals waiting to be rehomed. BOTTOM LEFT: An RSPCA vet examines a Yorkshire Terrier puppy.

Biology

Exaggerated features

Many breeds have been bred to emphasize certain physical features that, over time, have become more exaggerated. Although these may be 'normal' for a breed, flat faces, heavy wrinkles and very floppy ears are just a few examples of features that may cause problems.

For example, dogs with short, flat faces often have narrow nostrils and tiny windpipes. They can suffer severe breathing problems and may even have difficulty enjoying a walk or playing. Folded or wrinkled skin may be itchy and painful, and infolding eyelids can scratch the eyeball. Some of these problems will require

lifelong medication and sometimes surgery, so try to ensure that any puppy you choose is free from any exaggerated features.

Head and eyes

Selective breeding has resulted in variations ranging from the more elongated eyes of the

long-nosed dogs, such as the Greyhound and Collie, to the bulging eyes of some short-faced breeds, such as the Pug and Pekingese.

If you are unsure whether a puppy you have seen is healthy, always ask a vet for advice before buying the puppy.

Ears

Some breeds of dog have been selected to have large, floppy ears that dangle into things the dog investigates and are prone to damage and infection. Some dogs have folded ears, which can prevent good ventilation of the ear canal and also sometimes cause problems. Because ears are important for helping dogs communicate, having floppy or folded ears can make this difficult.

Teeth and teething

Most puppies are born toothless, although the outline of their teeth can be seen in the gums. By the time a puppy is 8 weeks old they will have a full set of 28 deciduous or milk teeth. By the age of 8 months, when teething is complete, a dog has 42 teeth.

Teething can be painful for puppies, and many will try to relieve their sore gums by chewing. Always provide your puppy with lots of safe toys and chews. As well as relieving soreness, chewing can also encourage the milk teeth to fall out. If they are not shed, milk teeth may have to be extracted to ensure that the permanent teeth are not displaced. This will also prevent infections due to food getting trapped between the milk and permanent teeth. Watch for signs of infection as this will need veterinary treatment.

Tail docking

Tail docking involves removing a puppy's tail, either by cutting it off or using a tight rubber band to make it die. Docking causes pain, and may also lead to long-term health problems and even death in some puppies. It can also affect a puppy's ability to communicate with other dogs. The law bans tail docking in England, Wales and Northern Ireland except under certain conditions and only when performed by a vet. There is a total ban in Scotland. If a puppy's tail is docked, the vet who does it must give the breeder a signed certificate to show that it has been done legally.

Claws

A puppy's nails should not be clipped while they are very young. Once allowed out, after vaccination, the puppy will usually wear down its own claws naturally by exercising on hard ground and pavements. If clipped before this, there is a tendency for the claws to lose their curvature and grow straight. Split and fractured claws can cause bleeding, tenderness and infection of the nail-bed, and should be treated by a vet.

LEFT: Labrador Retriever.

Environment

1

A suitable place to live

Before your puppy comes home, make sure you have prepared a suitable, safe place for them to live and that you have everything they will need to be happy and well looked after. Some things to consider:

Space

When they're not having fun playing or out on a walk, dogs and puppies need a comfortable, dry, draught-free, clean and quiet place to snooze in, as well as somewhere they can hide to avoid things that scare them. Giving your puppy a space of their own where they can have some privacy is really important, as your pet will need some quiet times alone in a place where they are not disturbed.

This can be difficult for a family with a new puppy, but make sure that everyone, especially children, knows that the puppy needs some space.

TOP: A Beagle crossbreed puppy enjoying some quiet time. ABOVE: Crates can provide a puppy with a safe place where they feel secure.

ABOVE: Make sure your puppy's bed is large enough for him or her to lie comfortably. RIGHT: Black Labrador puppy chewing on a ball.

Dog crates

Dog crates are widely available and can provide an open 'den' area that some puppies like to use as a safe place where they feel secure. They can also be used as a training aid both to help puppies learn to be left alone and to assist with toilet training. Note that crates should never be used as a punishment or to prevent unwanted behaviour. Sometimes a vet may advise the use of a crate to help recovery after surgery, and they can also be used to keep puppies secure and comfortable while they are travelling. You can find more information about using dog crates at www.rspca.org.uk/dogs/environment.

Keeping dogs outside

The RSPCA advises against keeping dogs and puppies outside because it can be very difficult to meet their needs. Living in a cold or wet place can cause a dog to suffer and may lead to illness. You might be thinking of keeping your dog outside because of a behaviour problem, such as toilet training or chewing, that is preventing you keeping them in the house. If this is the case, always talk to your vet first to rule out any underlying health issues. You may then be referred to a clinical animal behaviourist for further help. For more information on clinical animal behaviourists see page 47. If you still want to keep your dog outside, you can find out more about how to keep him or her healthy and happy at www.rspca.org.uk/dogs.

A suitable bed

Your puppy will need a comfortable place in which to rest and relax. Always look for a bed that is big enough to allow your pet to lie comfortably in natural positions, such as with their legs extended or curled up. Your puppy should also be able to go through the natural routine of turning around before settling. As well as being soft and padded, the bed should also be durable, washable and easy to dry so you can keep it clean. Make sure it is the right size and made of material that is safe for your dog. 'Bean bag' beds or foam bags, for example, could cause a problem if the puppy chews on it and chokes on the filling.

TOYS, EXERCISE & ACTIVITIES

Dogs are intelligent creatures, so if they get bored and do not have enough to do they can suffer. You need to make sure your puppy can exercise outdoors every day, and play and interact with people or other vaccinated, healthy, calm dogs. Your puppy will be inquisitive and playful so you will need to ensure there are always plenty of entertaining toys available for them to chew and play with.

Toys are important for all dogs – they can provide mental stimulation, physical exercise and can also help you to bond with your puppy. There are many types of toy on the market, including balls, soft toys, ropes for tugging, frisbees and squeaky toys. Each puppy will have their own preferences, but it is a good idea to have a variety of toys to keep playtime interesting and fun. Remember to check that toys are suitably sized for your puppy, to minimize the risk of smaller items being swallowed or choked on.

If you have more than one dog, make sure there are enough toys, beds and hiding places to go round to reduce the chances of your dogs becoming competitive and fighting. Choose toys for your puppy with care, avoid any with sharp edges and always replace them when damaged to avoid any chance of injury.

Transporting your puppy

It is very important to think about how you will transport your puppy safely. There are several options, so make sure you have decided how you will bring your puppy home and bought any necessary equipment before you collect them. Whichever method you choose, your puppy needs to be comfortable and it is up to you to ensure that they are safe in your vehicle.

Crate or harness?

Travelling crates and containers are popular. Make sure that your puppy has enough room to sit and stand up at full height, turn around easily and lie down in a natural position. You should also ensure that they can see out of the container and that there is enough ventilation and airflow. Suitable bedding should be placed on the floor to prevent the puppy from slipping around during the journey.

You could also consider using a car harness that secures your puppy by linking in with your car's seatbelt system. You will need to measure your dog and buy a harness of the right size. Always follow the instructions and ensure that the harness fits correctly. Remember that you may need to replace the harness when your puppy grows bigger. For more information go to www.rspca.org.uk/dogs/environment. If your puppy is going to travel on one of your car seats, you may also want to think about getting seat covers. These are especially useful when your puppy has been on a muddy walk.

Make sure your puppy's car harness fits properly – remember to check it regularly as they grow.

GENERAL TRAVEL TIPS

If you go on a long journey, make sure your puppy has regular stops to have a drink, exercise and go to the toilet.

It can get unbearably hot in a car on a sunny day, even when it is not that warm. In fact, when it is 22°C/72°F outside, the temperature inside a car can soar to 47°C/117°F within 60 minutes. You should never leave a dog alone in a car. Unlike humans, dogs pant to help keep themselves cool. In a hot, stuffy car dogs cannot cool down, and leaving a window open or a sunshield on your windscreen is not enough. The bottom line is that dogs can suffer terribly and even die in hot cars.

Diet

2

Heavy ceramic or metallic bowls are ideal for your puppy.

What to feed your puppy

A healthy diet

To stay fit and healthy, your puppy needs a well-balanced diet and constant access to fresh, clean water. How often and how much they need to eat will depend on things such as age, activity levels and general health. Your puppy's needs will also change as they grow. Unless your vet advises otherwise, adult dogs should be fed at least once a day. If you have any concerns or queries about feeding, your vet will be able to give you detailed advice on what – and how much – to feed your puppy.

Bowls

Before you bring your puppy home you will need to buy bowls for food and water. Your puppy will need separate bowls for eating and drinking. Make sure that your puppy's food and water bowls are kept clean by washing them every day. ▶

◀ The best bowls are durable and easy to clean – heavy ceramic or metal bowls are ideal as they are difficult to knock over and your puppy will not end up 'chasing' the bowls across the kitchen floor.

It is very important to ensure that the bowls are suitably sized for your puppy. The right size of bowl will depend on the size of your puppy, but if you use a food bowl that is meant for an adult dog take care not to overfill it. Overfeeding your puppy can lead to weight gain and health issues. You can find out more about obesity on page 41 and checks to make sure your puppy is a healthy weight on page 25.

Types of food

Puppies should be fed a weighed or measured amount of food at regular times. Dog food can be wet or dry, and what is suitable will depend on your individual puppy's needs. Meal times should always be supervised. Whatever prepared food you choose, always read the manufacturer's instructions. If your puppy is on a balanced diet that suits them, then stick to it unless your vet advises otherwise. If you do need to change your puppy's food, make sure that this is done gradually, otherwise they could end up with an upset stomach.

Water

Make sure that your puppy has constant access to fresh, clean drinking water. If your puppy is being fed a diet of dried food, this can make them very thirsty, so keep a close eye on their water bowl to ensure that it is kept topped up.

The first few days

A breeder or rescue centre will usually provide detailed information about a puppy's diet that will tell you what type of food they have been eating and how often. This is another reason why it is useful to ask a seller to fill out a puppy information pack, which is available to download at www.puppycontract. org.uk. This will prompt them to fill in background details about the puppy's current weight and information about their diet, so you will know what their feeding routine is and what type of puppy food they have been eating. It is also a good idea to ask for a few days' supply of food for your puppy.

Whenever possible, keep your puppy's food and feeding routine the same while they are settling in. Any changes to a puppy's diet should be made gradually because a sudden substitution in brand or type of food can lead to an upset stomach. Any change to a new food should be done over 4–5 days, with increasing amounts of the new food replacing the previous food each day.

Feeding balls, toys and Kongs

There are lots of different feeding toys available that require your puppy to work for their food. They are great tools for adding variety to your puppy's feeding routine, providing them with mental stimulation and also helping to keep your puppy occupied while you are out. Feeding toys range from Kongs and treat balls to more complex puzzle feeders. To make your puppy's mealtime more interesting you can fill a feeding toy such as a ball or Kong with food. This will keep your puppy busy as they chew, lick or shake the toy to get to the food.

Treats

Treats have an invaluable role to play in training your puppy, and a reward is sometimes appropriate at other times, too. Dog treats ▶

TOP LEFT: A Kong or feeding ball can make a puppy's mealtime more interesting. LEFT: Your puppy needs access to clean, fresh water at all times. FAR LEFT: RSPCA super premium puppy food.

can be purchased from a variety of shops, but do make sure they are suitable for your puppy and do not be tempted to give too many treats, as this can lead to weight gain. Take the treats out of your puppy's daily food allowance to avoid overfeeding.

Most puppies will try to beg titbits from the family but, however hard they are to resist, it is best not to feed your puppy from the table. It is always difficult to restrain children from sharing their sweets and crisps with their family pet, but remember that some human foods are poisonous to dogs (see page 42).

Human food

Most human meals don't provide dogs with the nutrition they need. Some foods, including chocolate, grapes, raisins and onions, as well as leftovers, can be poisonous to dogs (see page 42 for more information). It is best, therefore, to only give your puppy food that is specifically produced to give them a balanced and healthy diet.

Vegetarian food

If a puppy is to be fed on a vegetarian diet, it must be well balanced to ensure that they do not miss out on the nutrients that dogs need to stay healthy. An individual puppy's dietary needs will depend on their age, lifestyle and general health. If you are thinking of changing your puppy's diet, always consult your vet first.

Bones

Chewing is a natural and enjoyable behaviour for dogs, so it is important that they have safe, suitable objects to chew on. It is particularly important for teething puppies, as it helps their milk teeth fall out naturally and also gives some relief from the discomfort they may have when their permanent teeth are coming through.

There are concerns over the safety of giving bones to dogs and puppies for a number of reasons, including the risk of damage to their teeth, and the danger of choking or suffering an obstruction if bits of the bone splinter off. There is a range of manufactured toys and bones available that can be used as a safer substitute for bones and your puppy will enjoy chewing on them.

TOP LEFT: Beagle crossbreed puppy chewing on a Nylabone chew. LEFT: To avoid weight gain, treats should be taken from your puppy's daily food allowance. RIGHT: If you are concerned about your dog's weight, ask your vet for advice.

WEIGHT WATCH

There are a few simple regular checks you can make to help prevent your dog from becoming overweight:

- Make sure you can see and feel the outline of your dog's ribs without excess fat covering.
- You should be able to see and feel your dog's waist and it should be clearly visible when viewed from above.
- Your dog's belly should be tucked up when viewed from the side.

If your dog does not pass all three checks or if you are in any doubt about their weight, then talk to your vet. For further information about pet obesity visit the RSPCA website at www.rspca.org.uk/pets.

Behaviour

3

Regular exercise helps your dog to stay fit, as well as providing mental stimulation.

Puppy behaviour

Puppies are playful animals and enjoy having fun with toys, people and other dogs. They need to be able to behave normally, with regular exercise and plenty of opportunities to walk, run, play outdoors and learn new skills through training. Young puppies use enormous amounts of energy in play, so they also need plenty of time to sleep in their safe space – whether it is an open crate or their bed – where they will be undisturbed by children or the household routine.

Socialization and habituation

The first 14 weeks of a puppy's life are very important because during this time they learn most readily about the characteristics of dogs, other animals ▶

Training your puppy using rewards will help you to build a good relationship. BELOW: Having a well-trained dog will make life more enjoyable for you both.

and human beings they come into contact with. Lack of social contact during this period increases the risk of behaviours associated with fear and/or anxiety later in life. Puppies who have had positive experience of lots of types of people are less likely to be wary when they are handled or approached, and are more likely to grow up to be friendly and happy with people and animals.

They will take different situations in their stride, which is better for their stress levels and those of their new owners.

Puppies also need to be gradually introduced to a full range of normal household sounds and things that they will encounter in their new homes, such as vacuum cleaners, so that they learn not to be afraid of them.

Introduce a collar and lead gradually to help your puppy get used to them.

Keeping fit

Puppies need regular exercise to keep them fit, active and stimulated. How much exercise and the type of exercise your puppy needs will largely depend on their individual habits, age and health.

As well as being regularly walked, your puppy should also have a chance to run outdoors every day unless your vet recommends otherwise. For some types of puppy it is important that they are not over-exercised in their first year before their skeleton matures. If you are unsure about any aspect of exercising your puppy, ask your vet for advice.

Part of responsible dog ownership is making sure that you pick up and dispose of your puppy's faeces, whether in your garden or in a public place, as they can be a health hazard.

Training

Teaching your dog some basic cues, such as 'Sit', 'Down' and 'Come', is part of responsible dog ownership. Training is also a great way to spend time with your dog and provides them with important mental stimulation.

Train your puppy from an early age using rewards. Always try to be calm and consistent in the way you, your family and friends react to your dog. Training should always be fun – using rewards such as food and toys is the best way to motivate and teach your puppy. Never shout at or punish your puppy as they are very unlikely to understand and may become nervous or scared of you. Techniques that rely on inducing pain or fear are unnecessary to train puppies. They can lead to anxiety, upset the relationship between you and your dog, and may lead to behaviour problems.

Ask your vet for details of good local training classes that use kind, reward-based methods of training so that you can learn how to teach your puppy the skills they will need for everyday life. If your dog often shows fear or signs of stress, such as excessive panting, licking lips, hiding, cowering and aggression, or exhibits any other behaviour problems, talk to your vet. They can rule out any health problems that could be causing the issue and refer you to a clinical animal behaviourist if necessary.

House training

This is one of the first types of training your puppy will need. Puppies urinate frequently, and success in house-training depends on anticipating their needs, which are very predictable at an early age. Take your puppy outside every time they wake up, after play and eating or drinking. Depending on the puppy's age this may need to be as frequent as every hour. ▶

◀ Make sure you go with your puppy outside so that you can praise them when they go to the toilet in the correct place. Remember that toilet training your puppy will take time and patience. Some puppies are house trained quickly; others may take longer. For more detailed information go to www.rspca.org.uk/adviceandwelfare/pets/dogs/behaviour.

Collar and lead

By law, dogs must wear a collar and tag in public places, so your puppy will need to get used to wearing one. A correctly fitted collar should give room for two fingers to slip between the collar and the neck. It will need replacing when your puppy grows bigger, so you should regularly check that it still fits them.

It is important that the collar and lead are introduced gradually. A flat collar should be used, as other types such as choke chains, half-check chains and prong/pinch collars can cause pain and discomfort. These should not be used.

Your puppy needs to be taught how to walk on a lead or harness. In towns a lead or harness will offer protection from traffic and enable you to keep your puppy away from places where young children play. Even in the countryside, no matter how placid your dog is, use a lead when walking near livestock such as sheep and cows, which can often be the target of attacks by dogs. But try to find a safe area where you can let your dog off the lead for a good runaround.

When there are problems

The way a dog behaves depends on their age, type, personality and past experiences; frightening experiences and punishment can lead to behaviour problems and suffering. You should make sure your puppy has constant access to a safe hiding place to which they can escape if they feel afraid. If your puppy's behaviour changes, it could mean they are distressed, bored, ill or injured, so always talk to your vet if you are concerned. If necessary, your vet can refer you to a clinical animal behaviourist. For further information on clinical animal behaviourists, see page 47.

Barking

Dogs bark for a variety of reasons, such as during play, as a greeting or for attention. Prolonged periods of barking, however, may be a sign that your puppy is unhappy, so it is vital to find out why this is happening. If your puppy barks a lot when left alone, they may be having difficulty coping without you. It is important to talk to your vet, who may suggest referral to a clinical animal behaviourist. They can diagnose the root cause of the behaviour problem and develop a treatment programme, based on kind, reward-based methods, specifically for you and your puppy. You can find out more about behaviour problems at www.rspca.org.uk/dogs/behaviour.

Aggression

Dogs are usually aggressive in response to unfolding events, invariably because they think that they are under some form of threat. This could be a threat to their personal safety, when something or someone they value highly is taken away, or when they feel that their territory is threatened.

Dogs communicate mainly through body language. They have a wide range of non-aggressive signals and postures that they exhibit when they want us to stop doing whatever it is that they do not like. These include gestures that show they are uncomfortable, such as yawning, lip-licking, averting their gaze, turning their head away, dropping their ears, crouching low, wagging or tucking their tail under, and rolling over on their back. If these signals fail to work, the dog may then start to become more aggressive.

If your puppy shows signs of aggression, first, stop whatever it is that you are doing. Aggression is your puppy's way of warning you to stop. Second, stand still. Movement towards an aggressive puppy may be interpreted as a threat, and movement away may make him or her bold enough to bite. Stand still until the aggression stops, or walk slowly away, backwards or sideways, looking down and sideways. Talk to your puppy reassuringly. When the aggression stops, think about what caused it and avoid doing the same thing again. Puppies should never be punished for showing aggressive behaviour as this is likely to make them more fearful. If your puppy ever shows fearful or aggressive behaviour, get some professional advice. Talk to your vet, who will be able to refer you to a clinical animal behaviourist (see page 47). Our fact sheet on canine aggression, including information on where to go for help and advice, is at www.rspca.org.uk/adviceandwelfare/pets/dogs/behaviour/aggression.

Company

4

Dogs are sociable animals. Make sure your puppy has plenty of chances to interact with other friendly dogs.

Being with others

Dogs are sociable animals so they need and enjoy company. If they are treated well as puppies, they learn to see people as friends and companions.

Good company

If your puppy has pleasant experiences playing with a wide variety of other dogs early in life, it is more likely they will grow up to become a sociable dog. Providing your puppy is friendly towards other dogs, allow interaction with them on a regular basis. But if they are fearful of or aggressive towards other dogs, avoid the situations that lead to this behaviour and seek advice from a vet or clinical animal behaviourist (see page 47).

Never leave your puppy unsupervised with another animal or person who may deliberately or accidentally harm or frighten them. When you are away make sure your puppy is properly cared for by a responsible person.

If you have more than one dog, if possible house them together if they are friendly towards each other. Ensure they have enough space and can get away from one another if they want to, and that there are plenty of toys, water bowls and beds for each of them.

Friends for life

We all enjoy spending lots of time playing with and petting our puppies, but problems can arise if puppies become too dependent on human attention and get it 'on tap' when they are with us. If your puppy is worried about something and you always respond by giving attention, they may become anxious when left alone.

To avoid this so that you have a well-behaved and calm pet, you should follow some simple rules that are based on you deciding when to start and finish talking, petting or playing with him or her.

Unless you want a dog that constantly runs off with the remote control, jumps up at you or nudges your elbow, you should also ignore these unwanted behaviours. Instead, teach your puppy that sitting quietly is the best way to get your attention! For more detailed advice take a look at www.rspca.org.uk/dogs/company.

Learning to be left alone

One of the most effective ways of preventing your puppy from becoming anxious when they are left alone is to teach them right from the start that it can be enjoyable. To do this you need to very gradually increase the time that you leave your puppy alone, so that it is never frightening and always associated with something pleasant.

Try to always feed and exercise your puppy before leaving them. Take your puppy for a walk, returning home half an hour before you are due to leave. And give your puppy something to entertain them while you are away; this could be a 'special' toy or treat, such as a Kong stuffed with food. The speed at which you progress with this will depend on your puppy's reaction. Remember that if you leave your puppy without company and nothing to do for long periods of time they will become lonely, bored and distressed. Never leave your puppy for so long that they start to become anxious or upset. If you do have to go out and leave your puppy while they are very young, it is essential to arrange for friends or family to help out for a while.

Crossbreed puppies playing.
LEFT: Teach your puppy that
sitting quietly is the best way
to get your attention.

When there are problems

If you find there is a problem when you get home, it is vital that you do not react badly. Your puppy will link any punishment with your return rather than with the destruction, barking or toileting carried out some time earlier. They will then become anxious about what you will do when you return the next time you go out and, as a result, will be more likely to chew or lose toilet control, making the problem even worse!

Many puppies who have been punished in the past when their owners return will show certain behaviours in an attempt to appease them. They may make themselves as small as possible, putting their ears back and their tail between their legs. Unfortunately, owners often think that their pet is displaying this behaviour because they 'know they have done wrong'. Even if you take your dog to the scene of the 'crime', they will not be able to associate your anger with their behaviour hours earlier. All that will happen is that your puppy will simply become more anxious the next time you go out.

Although it is not easy, if you do find a mess when you come home please do not physically punish or shout at your puppy. Try to avoid letting your puppy see that you are annoyed. It is best to let them out into the garden while you clear up. Visit www.rspca.org.uk/dogseparation for further information.

Dogs and children

Many families with children keep dogs. Having a pet can improve a child's social skills, and caring for an animal can encourage kindness, understanding and responsibility. While children will quickly learn to treat a new puppy as part of the family, it is important to teach them to stay safe around dogs.

Golden rules for keeping your child safe and your dog happy

- Never leave your child alone in the same room as a dog, even your own.
- Teach your child never to approach dogs who: are eating or have a treat; have a toy or something else they really like; are sleeping; are unwell, injured or tired; are blind or deaf.
- Teach your child to be kind and polite to dogs. Do not let your child climb on dogs, pull their ears or do anything you would not allow them to do to another child.
- Teach your child how to play nicely with your dog. For example, your child can teach your dog some really fun tricks, such as 'shake a paw', 'play dead' or 'roll over'.
- Supervise your child when they are with your dog and never let them approach a dog they do not know, such as in the park.

A happy dog

Teach your child to recognize the signs of a happy dog who wants to meet you.

1 Dog has a relaxed body posture, smooth hair, mouth open and relaxed, ears in natural position, tail wagging, eyes normal shape.

2 Dog is inviting play with bottom raised, smooth hair, tail high and wagging, eyes normal shape, ears in natural position, may be barking excitedly.

3 Dog's weight is distributed across all four paws, smooth hair, tail wagging, face is interested and alert, mouth relaxed and open.

✓ TOP TIP

We all need a break sometimes – give your dog a cosy spot in a quiet room where they can have their own space. Teach your child to leave your dog alone when they are in their private spot.

A worried dog

These dogs are telling you that they are uncomfortable and do not want you to go near them.

1 Dog is standing but body posture and head position are low, tail tucked under, ears back and dog is yawning.

2 Dog is lying down and avoiding eye contact or turning head away from you and lip licking, ears back.

3 Dog is sitting with head lowered, ears back, tail tucked away, not making eye contact, yawning, raising a front paw.

An angry dog

These dogs are not happy and want you to stay away or go away.

1 Dog is standing with a stiffened body posture, weight forward, ears up, hair raised, eyes looking at you, pupils dark and enlarged, tail up and stiff, nose wrinkled.

2 Dog is lying down cowering, ears flat, teeth showing, tail down between legs.

3 Dog is standing with body down and weight towards the back, head tilted upwards, mouth tight, lips drawn back, teeth exposed, eyes staring, ears back and down, snarling.

Health
and welfare

5

If you have any concerns about your puppy's health, consult your vet.

Protecting your pet

Dogs can suffer from a range of diseases and other illnesses, but individual dogs show pain and suffering in different ways. A change in the way your puppy behaves can be an early sign that they are ill or in pain. Check your dog for signs of injury or illness every day, and make sure someone else does this if you are away.

Find a vet and arrange insurance

It is important that you find a vet to register your new puppy with, and book them in for a check-up and vaccinations. You can read more about finding a vet and low-cost vet care at www.rspca.org.uk/whatwedo/vetcare.

Check the insurance situation, too. Some charities and breeders may provide a short period of insurance cover, which you can either take over and extend, or you may want to arrange an alternative policy. Where insurance is not provided, it is a good idea to arrange for a policy to start as soon as you pick up the puppy.

Health checks

Take your dog for a routine health check with your vet at ▶

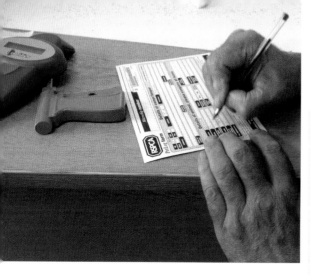

least once a year. It provides a good opportunity to ask for advice about things you can do to protect your dog's health, including essential vaccinations and treatments to control parasites (e.g. fleas and worms).

Microchipping

Microchipping your puppy gives them the best chance of being identified and returned to you if they are lost or stolen. A tiny microchip containing a unique code is inserted under their skin. This can be scanned and matched to your details, which are held on a database, so make sure you keep your contact information up to date.

Vaccinations

Vaccinations are very important to prevent certain deadly diseases, such as parvovirus. Puppies are normally vaccinated at around 8–10 weeks, but you should ask your vet for more information. If your puppy has been vaccinated

already, the vet will have given them a vaccination certificate that shows the vaccination date and products used. For more information go to www.rspca.org. uk/pets.

Worming

Regular worming is important for all puppies, as even healthy-looking animals can carry worms. Ask your vet about the best treatment to use, and how often. Avoid buying your puppy from breeders who have not wormed their dogs and puppies.

Fleas

If you have unexplained insect bites on your skin, or you notice your puppy scratching, they may have fleas. Check your puppy's fur carefully for dark specks or red-brown insects. If you find fleas, you must treat your pet and your home. Your vet can advise you on the best type of treatments to use; be aware that treatments suitable for dogs are not suitable for cats, and vice versa. Wash bedding, vacuum furniture, floors and skirting boards, and throw away the vacuum bag to get rid of any flea eggs. Flea problems must be tackled quickly, as fleas can infect your dog with the tapeworm parasite, as well as other diseases. Make sure your puppy is also wormed as part of the treatment.

Grooming

If grooming is introduced positively and slowly, it can be a great way of giving your pet some extra attention, developing and strengthening the bond between you, as well as performing the vital job of removing dirt and loose hair. It also provides an opportunity to carry out a health check: look for evidence of parasites such as fleas or ticks; check to see if your pet is the right weight; and notice any new or unusual lumps or bumps that might need further attention.

The amount of grooming a puppy needs depends on its coat type, but daily attention should be given to all puppies. If you are not sure how to groom your puppy's coat properly, talk to a pet-care specialist.

TOP LEFT: Microchipping helps to ensure your puppy can be identified if lost or stolen. ABOVE: Groom your puppy regularly to keep their coat in good condition. LEFT: Your vet can advise you which flea treatment is best for your puppy.

HEALTH ISSUES

Obesity

Obesity can cause serious health problems and shorten dogs' lives. Just as in humans, obesity in dogs can cause conditions such as diabetes, heart disease and high blood pressure. To protect your puppy from becoming obese, make sure they are fed a well-balanced diet and follow the simple checks on page 25.

Ear canal problems

Ear canal problems, one of the most common conditions seen in dogs, can have many causes, including mites, allergies and foreign bodies. Signs that your puppy might have a problem include scratching or rubbing their ears, or shaking their head. If you notice these symptoms, consult your vet promptly as ear conditions can be very painful and can cause long-term problems.

Diarrhoea and vomiting

Diarrhoea and vomiting is a very common condition in puppies. It may be due to the puppy having eaten unfamiliar or unsuitable food, or to an infection caused by bacteria or parasites. On rare occasions it may be caused by an obstruction in the intestine ▶

as a result of the puppy having swallowed a stone, marble or some other foreign body. Your vet will be able to advise on the best action to take if your puppy is affected.

Motion sickness

Many puppies are affected by motion sickness when travelling, with symptoms including nausea, drooling, vomiting and whining. Travelling can be quite stressful for dogs, so the symptoms may also be related to a fear of the car or being in it. Treats and rewards can help your puppy overcome their fear. Your vet will be able to give you more advice on how to help your puppy overcome the sickness.

Don't forget

Asking the breeder to fill out a puppy information pack when you get your puppy can help you to find out lots of useful information about their health.

Keeping your puppy safe in the home

Puppies are inquisitive and want to investigate the world in which they find themselves, but this can lead them into danger. Make sure that where your puppy lives is safe, secure and free from hazards. Before a new puppy is brought home, make sure you have taken steps to 'puppy-proof' your home. Ordinary household items, including pans of boiling water, hot fat, live cables, tablets, and toxic cleaners such as bleach are very dangerous for puppies and must therefore be kept well out of reach.

POISONING It is every responsible owner's nightmare that their pet might be poisoned. Make sure you are prepared for such an emergency. Preventing your dog from coming into contact with poisonous substances, and treating any accidental poisonings quickly and appropriately, are an important part of responsible pet ownership. Common items that are poisonous to dogs include chocolate, anti-inflammatory drugs such as ibuprofen, grapes/raisins/

sultanas/currants, slug and snail pellets and baits, weed killers and rodent poisons.

If you suspect that your pet has been poisoned, act quickly and immediately contact your nearest vet for advice. Signs of poisoning include vomiting, diarrhoea, dehydration, hyperactivity, high temperature and blood pressure, abnormal heart rhythm and tremors. There is more detailed advice on how to prevent poisonings at www.rspca.org.uk/poisoning.

HAZARDS IN THE GARDEN Before your puppy is allowed outside, check for hazards. Remove any ladders or other fixtures that give access to flat roofs or balconies. Garden ponds should be fenced off temporarily while the puppy is young. Take particular care to ensure your puppy is inside your car before driving off.

Check that your gates close securely and that they are constructed in such a way that a puppy cannot wriggle through them. Make sure that your children understand the importance of closing gates at all times, and urge this on regular visitors, too. In addition, check that fences and hedges are puppy-proof.

The electric flexes of garden equipment may look like tempting playthings to a puppy. Make sure your puppy is kept out of harm's way while garden equipment is in use. This applies to mowers, hedge-trimmers and similar items. Ensure that pesticides and other garden chemicals are stored out of reach, and check whether they are safe or toxic for animals; if in doubt ask your vet for advice.

IN AN EMERGENCY Emergencies can be really scary, but try not to panic.

- Stay calm. If you think your dog has been poisoned, remove them from the source of poison.
- Contact your vet for advice immediately. Always phone before taking your dog to the vet as they may be able to give you essential advice over the phone, and you may need to go to a different place than normal.
- Follow your vet's advice. If you are advised to take your dog to the vet, do so quickly and calmly.
- Never attempt to treat or medicate your dog yourself. Some medicines for humans and other animals may be poisonous to your dog.
- If you think your puppy has eaten something that will make them ill, never attempt to induce vomiting. Do not use salt water, as this is extremely dangerous.

CLOCKWISE FROM LEFT: Chocolate; slug pellets; household chemicals.

Your questions answered

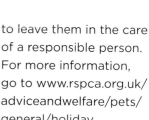

Lisa Richards BSc (Hons), dog behaviour and welfare expert,
Companion Animals Department, RSPCA.

Q: Since we got our puppy he's been really unsettled and nervous. How can we help him feel more secure?

A: It is important to give your puppy plenty of time to adjust and settle into your home. The change of environment might have been very stressful for him, so be patient and always avoid shouting at your puppy as it could make him afraid of you. There are lots of tips in this book about providing your puppy with a comfortable environment and suitable company, and helping to keep him happy and healthy. If you are concerned, it is best to get him checked by your vet first to rule out any illness or injury that could be causing the problem. Your vet can give you advice and if they feel it necessary might refer you to a clinical animal behaviourist. A behaviourist will work to identify the cause of the problem and then develop structured treatment plans that are suitable for you, your dog and your circumstances. Find out more at www.rspca.org.uk/findabehaviourist.

Q: We're going on holiday soon. Is it OK to take our puppy with us?

A: It's great to consider your puppy in your holiday plans. If you want to take your puppy with you, make sure you've checked with a vet that they're healthy to travel, and that your destination is pet-friendly. If you think your puppy might find the travelling and the change of environment stressful, it might be best to leave them in the care of a responsible person. For more information, go to www.rspca.org.uk/adviceandwelfare/pets/general/holiday.

Q: Should I brush my puppy's teeth?

A: Looking after our dogs' teeth is just as important as looking after our own! Dental disease is really common in dogs and can often need surgery or other treatment. Just like with humans, prevention is key, and all puppies will benefit from getting used to having their teeth cleaned with regular brushing from an early age to keep their teeth healthy. Without healthy teeth and gums dogs can develop bad breath, suffer from pain and can have trouble chewing their food.

Help keep your puppy's teeth healthy with regular brushing.

Q: Why does my puppy need pet insurance and microchipping?
A: You'll be covered for unexpected vet's bills in the future and safeguard your pet's health. Your dog will also get prompt veterinary care if injured. A one-off payment for microchipping your dog means you're more likely to be quickly reunited if they go missing. Don't forget that even if your dog is microchipped, they must still wear a collar and a tag engraved with your name and contact details.

Q: My puppy has been given tablets by the vet. How can I make sure she takes them?
A: The easiest way to get your puppy to take tablets is by hiding them in a treat. If she has to take several tablets a day, you may find it easier to buy a commercial pill-hiding product. Although sometimes costly, they can make taking the medicine less problematic for everyone. Your vet will be able to advise you on what foods are suitable to hide your puppy's tablets in, as well as other ways of encouraging her to take her medication. It is also important to only use medicines that have been prescribed for your individual puppy.

Index

Resources

RSPCA

For more information and advice from the RSPCA about caring for your puppy, go to www.rspca.org.uk/dogs.

Veterinary advice

- Advice on finding low-cost veterinary care: www.rspca.org.uk/findavet
- Vet Help Direct: www.vethelpdirect.com
- Vetfone: www.vetfone.co.uk. (24-hour service)
- Find a Vet: www.findavet.rcvs.org.uk/home

Dog trainers

- Find a dog trainer: www.rspca.org.uk/adviceandwelfare/pets/dogs/behaviour/trainer
- The Association of Pet Dog Trainers, UK (APDT): www.apdt.co.uk

Behaviour advice

- Advice on finding a behaviourist: www.rspca.org.uk/findabehaviourist
- The Association for the Study of Animal Behaviour (ASAB): www.asab.org
- The Association of Pet Behaviour Counsellors (APBC): www.apbc.org.uk

- If you are concerned about your puppy's behaviour, contact a major rescue organization or rehoming centre, such as the RSPCA, for expert advice. They will be happy to help you, even if you have not adopted your pet from their rehoming centres.

Information on inherited diseases in dogs

- Get Puppy Smart: www.getpuppysmart.com
- The Puppy Contract: www.puppycontract.org.uk
- Dog Breed Health: www.dogbreedhealth.com
- University of Cambridge Inherited Diseases in Dogs Database: www.vet.cam.ac.uk/idid
- Universities Federation for Animal Welfare: www.ufaw.org.uk/dogs.php
- Canine Inherited Orders Database: www.upei.ca/cidd
- University of Sydney: www.vetsci.usyd.edu.au/lida

PET GUIDE

Learn more about other popular pets with these bestselling RSPCA pet guides

Care for Your Guinea Pigs

Find out what your guinea pigs need to stay happy and healthy

Care for Your Hamster

Find out what your hamster needs to stay happy and healthy

Care for Your Rabbits

Find out what your rabbits need to stay happy and healthy

Care for Your Kitten

Find out what your kitten needs to stay happy and healthy